The A to Z of Irish Crime

The A to Z of Irish Crime

A Guide to Criminal Slang

Edited by John Mooney and Jean Harrington

PUBLISHED BY MAVERICK HOUSE PUBLISHERS.

Maverick House, Office 19, Dunboyne Business Park,
Dunboyne, Co. Meath, Ireland.

Maverick House Asia, Level 43, United Centre, 323 Silom Road,
Bangrak, Bangkok 10500, Thailand.

info@maverickhouse.com
http://www.maverickhouse.com

ISBN: 978-1-905379-12-5
10 digit ISBN: 1-905379-12-9

5 4 3 2 1

The paper used in this book comes from wood pulp of
managed forests. For every tree felled, at least one tree is
planted, thereby renewing natural resources.

A CIP catalogue record for this book is available from the
British Library.

Introduction

There are already many books in print on the use of slang in Western society, and how it varies from region to region. This is the first book that deals specifically with Irish criminal slang, which can often differ greatly from American slang, and even differs from our nearest neighbours in Britain.

While most of the terms find their origins in the criminal community, as language continually mutates and changes, many of the terms are also used in common parlance.

Words like 'dough' and 'bread' were once used exclusively in criminal circles, but now are commonly used in everyday speech amongst the masses. These words form part of this A to Z.

Irish criminal slang tends not to use terminology from the US, despite the fact that our language in general is becoming more Americanised as a result of what the experts call the 'MTV effect'.

Rhyming slang from Britain has also been slow to be picked up in Ireland. While the 'Peggy Dell' (smell) may be 'Padraig Pearse' (fierce) in parts of Dublin, it's rare to hear someone say they'll take the 'apple and pears' (stairs) instead of the lift. Whereas a 'skydiver' was appropriate for an Irish fiver, it doesn't have the same ring when referring to a five-euro note.

There are likely to be arguments about the use of the words included in this book. People in Belfast don't use slang in the same way as people from Cork, so it's possible that readers may not have heard all the words in common usage.

Slang interpretation can never be an exact science, but we welcome feedback from readers who have alternate meanings for words that are used here, or feel that some slang has been omitted in error.

J. Harrington & J. Mooney, 2008.

Acknowledgements

Special thanks to Alan Sherry who was involved at the concept stage of the book, and who contributed greatly as it developed.

A BIG ASK; a big favour.

A BIT ON THE SIDE; a mistress or boyfriend outside of the main relationship.

A FEW BOB; money.

A GOOD ROGERING; to have great sex.

ACE; excellent at crime.

ACE IN THE HOLE; to keep something in reserve.

ACID; street slang for LSD, a hallucinogenic drug.

ACTION; to engage in crime, gun crime or terrorism.

ACTIVE SERVICE UNIT; term applied to paramilitary units actively engaged in terrorism.

ADAM AND EVE; a type of ecstasy.

AFRICAN BLACK; cannabis.

AFRICAN SALAD; khat, a drug used by African immigrants.

AIR BAGS; enhanced or fake breasts.

AIRVENT; gunshot injury to the head.

AK-47 OR AK; street name for the AK-47 assault rifle, which was originally designed by Mikhail Kalashnikov.

ALADDIN'S CAVE; location where stolen property or contraband is stored.

ALIAS; false identity used by criminals.

ALIBI; someone who is willing to lie to protect an associate.

ANGEL DUST; cattle growth promoter.

ANIMAL; someone who is dangerous and displays psychopathic intentions towards his enemies.

ANVIL; Operation Anvil, an ongoing intelligence-led policing operation which targets those involved in gangland crime in the Dublin region.

APACHE; someone who is considered to be dangerous and unpredictable.

APPLES; breasts.

ARMY, THE; the Provisional IRA.

ARSE BANDIT; a derogatory term for a homosexual.

ARSEWIPE; a fool.

ASBO; Anti-social behaviour order.

ATM; Automated Transaction Machine.

AUL MAN; a father.

AUL ONE; a mother.

AWAY; to be on the run abroad, or in prison.

AWOL; absent without leave.

BACK–UP; reinforcements.

BACKTRACK; term used by heroin addicts: to allow blood from a vein to flow into a syringe.

BAD TRIP; an experience using drugs that requires medical assistance.

BAGMAN; a money launderer.

BAIL; to be freed on bail.

BALE; term used to describe a kilo of cannabis.

BANG, TO; to have sex.

BANGED UP; to be incarcerated or sent to prison.

BANGED TO RIGHTS; a criminal who is caught red-handed.

BAR; term used to describe cannabis.

BARBS; barbiturates.

BAREBACK RIDING; having unprotected sex.

BATTER, ON THE; to get drunk, to go drinking.

BEAK; a judge.

BEAMER; a BMW car.

BEAT; garda division.

BEAT COP; a uniformed garda officer.

BEAT, TO; to win.

BEAVER; vagina.

BENDER; a suspended sentence.

BENDER, TO GO ON A; to go wild on drink or drugs.

BENT; to be homosexual or corrupt.

BEVVY; an alcoholic drink.

BIG C; cocaine.

BIG MAN; a criminal boss.

BINGO; solved, or sorted.

BIRD; a prison sentence.

BITE ONE'S LIP, TO; to remain silent.

B.J., BLOW-JOB; oral sex performed on a man.

BLAG; to rob.

BLAGGER; an armed robber.

BLAST, TO; to shoot someone.

BLEED THEM DRY; to extort someone's money or cash reserves.

BLIND FENCE; innocent purchaser of stolen property or goods.

BLOW; cannabis resin, or herbal cannabis.

BLUE; pornography.

BLUFF; to engage in fraud.

BOGEY; someone who is untrustworthy and unreliable.

BOLTHOLE; a hideout.

BOMBED OUT; to be intoxicated.

BONER, A; an erection.

BOOK; book of evidence presented by prosecution to an accused person in advance of a criminal trial.

BOOKMAN; a garda officer who is tasked with compiling documents and statements for inclusion in a book of evidence.

BOTTLE; courage.

BRANCH, THE; nickname for Special Branch, a garda unit that combats terrorism.

BRASSER; a prostitute.

BREAD; money or cash derived from a robbery or some other form of criminal enterprise.

BRIDEWELL; district courts located to the rear of the Bridewell Garda Station in Dublin city.

BRIEF; a solicitor or barrister who specialises in criminal law.

BROWN; heroin.

BROWN BREAD; someone who has been murdered or has died.

BROWN ENVELOPE; a term for corrupt money. Refers to the system in which people would bribe politicians or planners by giving them cash in a brown envelope.

BUBBLY; champagne.

BUCKETS OF BLOOD; nickname applied to someone who exaggerates or is overly pessimistic.

BUG; an eavesdropping device which is attached to a telephone or telephone line or inserted into a vehicle.

BUGGED; a telephone line, car or room that has been compromised by gardaí.

BUMBOY, A; a male prostitute.

BUMMER, A; a bad experience with drugs.

BUM RAP; false allegation.

BUM'S RUSH; to show an adversary the door.

BUMP OFF; to kill.

BUMP UP; using cocaine to bolster ecstasy.

BURN, TO; to deceive someone.

BUSH; vagina.

BUSTED; to be caught.

BUZZ; a euphoric feeling caused by drug usage.

CAB; Criminal Assets Bureau.

CANARY; someone who informs on his associates or someone who co-operates with gardaí.

CANDYMAN; a cocaine dealer.

CARJACK; to rob a vehicle at gunpoint.

CARRY, TO; to carry a firearm.

CARVE UP, TO; to share the proceeds of a crime, or to attack an enemy with a knife.

CASE, TO; to reconnoitre a location for nefarious purposes, or to avoid detection.

CAT; a sneak-thief.

CHAMPAGNE AND CAVIAR; cocaine and cannabis.

CHARGED; to face criminal prosecution.

CHARGE SHEET; document used to press criminal charges.

CHARLIE; cocaine.

CHASE THE DRAGON; to smoke heroin from foil.

CHEAPSKATE; someone who refuses to pay his share of a bill.

CHICKENS; forged cheques.

CHICKEN SALAD; khat: a drug used mainly by African immigrants.

CHINA GIRL; a prostitute of Chinese origin.

CHINA WHITE; heroin.

CHIS; police slang for an informant. The word is an abbreviation of Covert Human Intelligence Source.

CHIV; a homemade knife or razor used by prison inmates.

CLAMP DOWN, TO; to suppress crime.

CLEAN; a drug addict who no longer uses. The word is sometimes applied to suspects who are unknown to gardaí.

CLOCK, TO; to recognise.

CLOUD NINE; crack cocaine.

COCKTAIL; a combination of drugs taken at once.

COKE; cocaine.

COKE PARTY; a party where cocaine is used.

COLD FEET; term applied to a criminal who backs out of participating in a crime or heist.

COLD TURKEY; to stop using drugs without the aid of medication.

COLOMBIAN; cocaine.

COME CLEAN, TO; to confess.

COME HEAVY, TO; to exert pressure.

CON; a fraud.

CONCERNED PARENTS; the Concerned Parents Against Drugs (CPAD). Members of local community groups who organised themselves to oppose heroin dealers.

CONFIDENCE MAN; a fraudster who gains the trust of a victim in order to defraud them.

CONMAN; a fraudster or former criminal.

CONNECT, TO; to purchase drugs.

CONTRABAND; term used to describe goods that are prohibited in a country or prison.

CONVICT; a person who has been found guilty of a crime.

COOLER; a prison.

COP; a garda officer or detective.

COP A PLEA, TO; to plead guilty or confess to gardaí.

COP OUT, TO; to avoid having a discussion.

COSTA, THE; the Costa Blanca or Costa del Sol, popular destinations for Irish criminals involved in arms trafficking, drug smuggling and money laundering.

CRACK; nickname for crack cocaine.

CRACKER, A; an attractive female.

CRASH, TO; to sleep off the effects of drugs.

CREEPER; a thief who breaks into homes or properties while the occupants are asleep or going about their work.

CREW; a gang.

CRUST; money. To earn a crust.

CRUSTY, A; a new age traveller.

CUT; to stab a rival.

CUT OUT; to leave someone out of a financial deal.

DAB; slang for fingerprints.

DABBLER; occasional drug user.

DAISY-CHAIN; a criminal who is handcuffed to two prison officers.

DAMAGED GOODS; a girl who isn't a virgin.

DEADBEAT; a person who doesn't pay their way.

DEADLY; brilliant.

DEAD MAN WALKING; someone whose life is under threat.

DEAD PICKER; a prostitute who robs drunken clients.

DEAD RINGER; a look alike. Someone who is the double of someone else.

DEAL; a small quantity of drugs, usually heroin.

DEALER; someone who sells drugs.

DEAR JOHN; a letter written to end a relationship.

DECK; a packet of cigarettes, or a small amount of drugs.

DECOY; a person who attempts to create a distraction in order to conceal a crime.

DESIGNER DRUGS; synthetic drugs.

D. I.; Detective Inspector.

DIP, TO; to pickpocket.

DIPPER; a pickpocket.

DIRT; gossip. To 'get the dirt on somone.'

DISCO BISCUITS; ecstasy tablets.

DITCH; to get rid of, to throw away.

D. O.; Detective Officer.

D.O.A; dead on arrival.

DO A RUNNER; to flee a garda investigation.

DO THE BUSINESS; to commit a crime without getting caught. Someone who can be relied upon to do the business.

DO TIME; to serve a jail sentence. To go to jail.

DOG'S BOLLOX; fantastic. 'He thinks he's the dog's bollox.'

DOG'S LIFE; an unhappy life.

DOLL; a good-looking girl.

DOPE; cannabis.

DOPE HEAD; a drug addict.

DOSE, A; a sexually transmitted disease.

DOSH; money.

DOTS; LSD, a hallucinogenic drug.

DOUGH; money.

DOWNERS; prescription drugs.

DRAGGING AN ANCHOR; married.

DRAG-WEED; marijuana.

DREAM STICK; an opium pipe.

DRILL; to shoot someone.

DRIVE-BY; to shoot at someone from a car.

DROP, TO; to take a drug orally.

D. S.; Drugs Squad.

D.S.; Detective Sergeant.

DUBLIN CASTLE; nickname for the Garda National Drugs Unit which operates from Dublin Castle.

DUD, A; a pill that is passed off as an ecstasy tablet.

DUFF, UP THE; pregnant.

DUMMY-RUN; a practice run to ensure a plan runs smoothly.

DYKE, A; a lesbian.

E; ecstasy.

EAGER BEAVER; a young criminal recruit who cannot wait to get started.

EARNER, A NICE LITTLE; a crime that could earn a lot of money.

EASY GRAFT; an easy way to make money.

EASY STREET; having plenty of money.

EAT; to take acid or mushrooms.

EAT OUT; to perform cunnilingus.

EFFING AND BLINDING; cursing non-stop.

ELBOW, TO GET THE; to be discharged or dismissed.

ELIMINATE; to kill someone.

ENFORCER; a gunman sent by a gang to kill or intimidate rivals.

EQUALISER; a gun.

ERASE; to kill someone.

ERU; the Emergency Response Unit, a specialist armed intervention unit that works within the Special Detective Unit (SDU) of An Garda Síochána.

E-TARD; someone who is under the influence of ecstasy.

EUROPOL; the European Police Organisation.

EVE; ecstasy.

EVEN BREAK; a good deal, one where no one is cheated.

EVEN-STEVEN; fifty-fifty, or on equal terms.

EVEN THE SCORE; to seek revenge on someone.

EXPERIENCE; the experience of using drugs.

EYEBALL; to stare at someone.

EYEWASH; nonsense.

FACE; a known criminal or figure in the underworld.

FACTORY; a secret location where drugs are manufactured.

FAG; a cigarette; a homosexual.

FAGGOT; derogatory term for a homosexual.

FAG-HAG; a woman who spends a lot of time with gay men.

FAIRY; an offensive word used to describe a homosexual.

FALL GUY; someone who takes the blame for another person's crime.

FANCY WOMAN; a mistress.

FEDS, THE; members of the Garda Federation.

FENCE; a criminal known to sell stolen goods.

FIELDS; LSD.

FINGER, TO; to identify criminals to gardaí.

FINGERSMITH; a pickpocket.

FINISHING SCHOOL; jail for women.

FIRM; a criminal gang.

FISH, TO; to look for information.

FITTER; a member of a gang who opens locks.

FIT-UP, TO; to plant false evidence or entrap.

FIVE-SPOT; a five-euro note; a five-year term in jail.

FIX, A; a deal of heroin.

FLAKES; cocaine.

FLASHBACK; to have a hallucination.

FLATLINE, TO; to die.

FLEECE, TO; to steal.

FLORIDA SNOW; cocaine.

FLUSH; having lots of money.

FLY A KITE; to smuggle a letter in or out of prison.

FLYING; to be under the influence of drugs.

FLYING IN THE CLOUDS; someone who is under the influence of drugs.

FOOTBALLS; amphetamine.

FOOT SOLDIER; a low-level member of a criminal gang.

FORGET-ME PILL; Rohypnol.

FRAME, IN THE; term applied to a person who is identified as a suspect.

FRAME, TO; to secure a conviction by planting false evidence on a suspect or at a location.

FREAK OUT, TO; to have an unexpected reaction to a drug.

FREEBASE; to smoke cocaine or crack.

FREEBIE; something that is given away for free.

FRENCH POLISH; term used by prostitutes to describe oral sex.

FROGS; French citizens.

FRONT, TO; a business person who represents a criminal gang to help them launder the proceeds of crime.

FUCK, TO; to have sex.

FUCK ABOUT, TO; to be a nuisance to others.

FUCK OFF, TO; to abscond abroad or to leave one's home.

FUCKED UP, TO BE; to be high on drugs.

FULL OF LEAD; someone who has been shot several times, i.e. 'They are full of lead.'

FUNERAL DIP; a pickpocket who specialises in robbing at funerals.

FUNNY FARM; a psychiatric institution.

FUZZ, THE; the Garda Síochána.

GAG, TO; to silence by way of a court injunction.

GAME; term used to describe dangerous dogs used in dogfighting or illegal blood sports.

GAME, ON THE; to engage in prostitution.

GANGBANG; a crime which involves multiple rapes.

GANGLAND; another term for the underworld.

GANGSTER; a career or professional criminal. The term is also used to describe someone who is dangerous.

GANJA; cannabis resin, or herbal cannabis.

GASU; code-name for the Garda Air Support Unit which became operational in September 1997.

G.B.H; grievous bodily harm.

GEAR; street slang for heroin.

GET CAUGHT, TO; to get pregnant.

GET TO; to intimidate or kill.

GHOST, A; a surveillance garda.

GIRLFRIEND; cocaine.

GIVE UP, TO; to surrender money or contraband to gardaí.

GLASS; diamonds.

GLASSHOUSE, THE; the military prison in the Curragh Camp in Co. Kildare.

GLUED; married.

GLUEY; someone who sniffs glue.

GO DOWN ON; to perform oral sex.

GOLD DUST; cocaine.

GOLDEN DRAGON; LSD, a hallucinogenic drug.

GOLDEN GIRL; heroin.

GONG; an opium pipe.

GOODS; stolen items; drugs.

GOOF; to get high on drugs, usually heroin.

GOOFBALL; cocaine and heroin taken together.

GOPHER; a low-ranking criminal who collects and delivers drugs.

GRAB; to arrest or detain a person suspected of committing a crime.

GRAFTER; a person who works for a living.

GRAM; an imperial weight of cocaine.

GRASS; a garda informer.

GREEN; inferior-quality marijuana.

GREEN GOODS; paper money.

GREEN LIGHT; signal to proceed.

GRILL; to question or interrogate.

GUN RUN; to smuggle arms.

GUTTER JUNKIE; an addict who relies on others to provide them with drugs.

H; a nickname for heroin.

HABIT; an addiction to drugs.

HACHETTE-MAN; a hired assassin or someone sent to inflict injury.

HACK; a journalist.

HANDJOB; masturbation performed by another person.

HANDLER; garda officer who operates informers in criminal gangs.

HANDOVER; a payment for drugs.

HAPPY PILL; ecstasy.

HARDMAN; someone with a reputation for violence.

HARDWARE; guns and weaponry.

HASH; cannabis resin.

HEAD; an associate of a criminal or criminal gang; also oral sex.

HEADBANGER, A; a criminal prone to unprovoked violence.

HEADSHOP; a store that sells legal herbal drugs and related paraphernalia.

HEAP; a wrecked car.

HEAT; to feel pressure.

HEAVY; a major criminal known to be violent or to have access to weapons.

HEIST; a robbery usually involving the use of guns.

HERB; herbal cannabis.

HIGH SOCIETY; professional people who use cocaine.

HIJACK, TO; to rob a lorry, usually at gunpoint.

HIP HOP; a type of music/art/fashion.

HIT; an assassination plot.

HIT MAN; a contract killer.

HME ; home-made explosives.

HOLE; a dwelling place that is in a state of disrepair.

HOLE, TO GET YOUR; to have sex with someone.

HOLE-IN-THE-WALL GANG; the nickname given to the criminal gang led by John Gilligan, a convicted drugs smuggler. The name is derived from the *modus operandi* used by the gang to enter warehouses to steal goods.

HOME-GROWN; locally grown herbal cannabis.

HOOCH; alcoholic drink made in prison by inmates.

HOOKER; a prostitute.

HORSE; heroin.

HOT ICE; stolen diamonds.

HOTSHOT; someone who thinks they are superior to others.

HUSTLE, TO; to defraud.

ICE; amphetamine.

ICE CUBE; crack cocaine.

ICE-CREAM HABIT; occasional drug use.

ICING; cocaine.

I.D.; identification.

IN; being on the inside of a deal; an entrance.

IN CAMERA; a court case which the public are prohibited from attending.

IN HOCK; to be in debt to a third party.

IN THE CAN; in jail.

IN THE CLEAR; free from suspicion or prosecution.

INCENSE; opium.

INDIAN BOY; cannabis.

INGRAM, AN; slang term for Ingram Sub-machine-gun, usually a MAC-10 model.

INLA; the Irish National Liberation Army, the military wing of the Irish Republican Socialist Party (IRSP).

INSIDE; in prison or being held on remand.

INSIDE JOB; when a crime is committed by someone known to the victim.

INTEL; security parlance for intelligence information.

IPLO; Irish People's Liberation Organisation, a paramilitary group formed in 1986 as a result of a feud between INLA members.

IRON BRACELETS; handcuffs.

IRPS; the Irish Republican Socialist Party, the political wing of the INLA.

JAG; a car manufactured by Jaguar.

JAILBAIT; a girl who is below the age of sexual consent.

JELLIES; a mixture of depressants and ecstasy.

JELLY; gelignite.

JIMMY; an iron bar used to break into premises.

JOB; a criminal operation, such as a bank job.

JOCKER, IN A; in a fix.

JOCKEY; a prostitute's client.

JOINT; a roll-it-yourself cigarette which contains cannabis.

JOY, THE; prison slang for Mountjoy Prison in Dublin.

JUICE; vaginal secretion.

JUMP, TO; to mug or attack a person.

JUMPER; a thief who jumps shop counters to steal or rob from cash registers.

JUNK; street name for heroin.

JUNKIE; a term used to describe a drug addict.

JUNKYARD; prison slang for Mountjoy Prison in Dublin.

K; ketamine. Also a kilo of a particular drug.

K-HOLE; a period of ketamine-induced confusion.

KAMIKAZE PILOT; someone who does not care about his own welfare.

KANGAROO COURT; a military tribunal set up by the IRA.

KET; ketamine.

KEVLAR; a light but strong synthetic fibre used to make bullet-proof vests.

KHAT; *Catha edulis*, a flowering plant native to Africa, which produces natural stimulant properties. It is used mainly by African immigrants.

KICK, TO; to stop using drugs.

KIP; street name for sleep.

KITE; a forged cheque or document.

KITING; to misrepresent a stolen cheque in order to defraud a bank or financial institution.

KIT-KAT; a type of ecstasy.

KNEECAPPING; to shoot a victim, usually through the knees. A form of punishment dispensed by paramilitaries.

KNOCK, TO; customs slang for seizing a drugs haul that is under surveillance.

KNOCK OFF; a fake product.

KNOCK UP; to get a woman pregnant.

KNOCKING SHOP; a brothel or massage parlour.

LACE, TO; to poison or contaminate.

LAG; a prisoner.

LAMP; to strike out at or attack; a fool, someone who is not clever.

LANDING; a prison landing.

LAUNDER; to turn the proceeds of crime into legitimate income.

LAUNDRY MAN; someone who launders money.

L.E.; liquid ecstasy.

LEATHER, TO; to beat someone senseless.

LEBANESE; cannabis resin.

LEBANESE LOOP; a device used to steal bank cards from ATM machines.

LEGGER, TO DO A; to run away.

LEMON; a fool or someone who is not very bright.

LEVEL, ON THE; to be honest with someone. To provide an honest account of an event.

LIFER; a prisoner who is serving a life sentence.

LINE, A; a line of cocaine.

LINE-UP; an identification parade organised by the gardaí.

LOAD, A; a consignment of drugs.

LOADED; weapon that contains live ammunition and is ready for use.

LOAN SHARK; an illegal money lender.

LOCKDOWN; the practice of confining inmates to their prison cells.

LOOT; the proceeds of a robbery or crime. It can refer to money or property.

LOVE DRUG; ecstasy.

LOVE TRIP; having sexual intercourse while using ecstasy.

LSD; a hallucinogenic drug.

MAC-10; a highly compact, selective-fire sub-machine-gun. The name is derived from an abbreviation of the Ingram Military Armament Corporation Model 10.

MADAME; a female proprietor of a brothel.

MAGIC MUSHROOMS; psilocybin mushrooms, which, when ingested, cause users to hallucinate.

MAINLINE; to inject heroin.

MDMA; methylenedioxymethamphetamine. The chemical name for ecstasy.

MEET, A; a meeting of criminals.

MELONS; breasts.

MET, THE; British police.

METHADONE; a pain reliever, similar to morphine. Methadone is used widely in Ireland in the treatment of heroin addiction, as it reduces withdrawal symptoms without causing the 'high' associated with heroin.

MINGER; someone who smells, or is considered physically unattractive.

MINOR; a person who is not an adult in the eyes of the law.

MITSUBISHI; a form of ecstasy.

MO; *Modus Operandi.*

MOLL, A; the girlfriend, wife or mistress of a criminal. A woman who wants to be seen with criminals attending societal functions.

MOONSTONE; a slice of MDMA mixed with a deal of heroin.

MORPHO; morphine.

MUG, TO; to rob or attack a pedestrian.

MUG SHOT; a photograph taken of a suspect while he or she is in police custody.

MULE; a drugs courier.

MUPPET; a fool or someone with no street sense.

MUSHROOMS; psilocybin mushrooms.

NAB, TO; to arrest or detain someone.

NAGGING; constant complaining.

NAIL, TO; to secure a conviction against a criminal.

NEEDLE; a syringe.

NICK; prison.

NIGHTHAWK, A; a criminal who operates at night.

NIPPERS; offspring or children.

NONCE; a child molester.

NOOKIE; sex.

NOSE CANDY; cocaine.

NOSE DROPS; liquified heroin.

NOSE POWDER; cocaine.

NSU; National Surveillance Unit, a garda unit which covertly monitors the activities of criminals and paramilitaries.

NUGGET; a piece of information.

NUT, TO; to murder someone.

NUT-HOUSE; a mental asylum.

NUTTER; someone who suffers from a psychiatric condition.

OBE; out-of-body experience.

OD; overdose.

OFF THE CUFF; an impromptu decision.

OFFICIALS, THE; the Official Irish Republican Army (OIRA).

OLD BILL; Irish criminal slang for the British police.

ON A TRIP, TO BE; under the influence of drugs.

ON THE GAME; to engage in prostitution.

ON THE JOB; committing a crime.

ON TOP, TO COME; a crime that has been uncovered by gardaí or customs as it is happening.

ONE-TRICK PONY; a person with just one talent.

OP; observation post.

OUNCE; a standard measure of cannabis.

OUT OF IT; to be under the influence of drugs.

OUTSIDE; prison slang for the outside world.

OVER THE WALL; to escape from prison.

PAD; a room or flat used to sleep in.

PADDING; the criminal practice of sewing drugs into the lining of clothes or baggage; embellishing a statement taken from a criminal.

PADRAIG PEARSE; fierce.

PAPER; an arrest warrant.

PARACHUTE DOWN; to take ecstasy after using heroin.

PATCH; a criminal territory used for the distribution of drugs.

PAY-OFF; a bribe or inducement.

PCP; phencyclidine, a prescription drug.

PEDIGREE; a criminal record or reputation.

PEELER; republican and IRA slang for gardaí.

PEEPER; garda slang for a criminal who derives sexual satisfaction from secretly watching women undress.

PEGGY DELL; smell.

PEPSI HABIT; to occasionally use drugs.

Peruvian; cocaine.

Pick-up; to purchase drugs.

Piece of work, a; an expression of either admiration or hatred for someone.

Pig; a garda officer.

Pikey; a member of the travelling community.

Pill, a; an ecstasy tablet.

Pimp; a person who lives off the immoral earnings of prostitution.

Pipebomb; an improvised explosive device.

Plant, a; a garda informant.

Plant, to; to plant evidence.

Plug, to; to murder or shoot someone.

Poke; money.

Poppers; amyl and buyl nitrate capsules, usually used by homosexual men during intercourse.

Pot; cannabis resin.

Pot-head; a regular cannabis user.

Prick tease; a girl who flirts with a man but has no intention of sleeping with him.

Pro, a; a professional.

Provos; the Provisional Irish Republican Army (PIRA).

Pump, to; to obtain information; to have sex.

Punter; a man who uses and pays for the services of prostitutes.

Puppies; breasts.

Put away; to be sent to jail.

Q; Dublin slang for a small measure of heroin.

Q.T., ON THE; on the quiet, without anyone knowing.

QUACK, A; a doctor.

QUARE ONE, THE; refers to one's girlfriend or wife.

QUARTER; a measure of cannabis resin or heroin.

QUAT; *Catha edulis*, a flowering plant native to Africa, which produces natural stimulant properties. It is used mainly by African immigrants. Also known as khat.

QUEER; a derogatory name for a homosexual man.

QUARTER MOON; cannabis.

QUICKY; casual sex.

QUILL; a barrister.

R-2; Rohypnol, a sedative.

RACKET; a criminal enterprise.

RAP, TO; to talk to someone.

RASTA; a Rastafarian.

RAT; an informer.

READY UP; a crime that has yet to happen but is already known to the police.

REALS, THE; the Real IRA (RIRA), a breakaway faction of the Provisional IRA.

RED EAGLE; heroin.

REEFER; a cigarette that contains cannabis.

RIDE, TO; to have sex with someone.

RINGER; a look alike.

RIRA; Real Irish Republican Army.

ROACH; part of a hand-rolled cigarette which acts as a filter.

ROCKET FUEL; PCP.

ROCKS; street name for crack cocaine. Also used for diamonds.

Rod; a gun.

RPGs; rocket-propelled grenades.

Rub out; to murder.

Rumble; to be discovered.

Rush, a; a sudden or intense surge of pleasure caused by ingesting ecstasy.

SACK, HIT THE; to go to bed.

SCAG; heroin.

SCANGER; a working-class person who wears tracksuits.

SCHROOMS; psilocybin mushrooms.

SCOPE, TO; to carefully survey a place.

SCORE, TO; to purchase drugs.

SCREW; a prison officer.

SCROTE; a derogatory term for a young person.

SCUMBAG; a person of disrepute.

SEMMY; Semtex plastic explosive.

SET-UP, TO BE; to be betrayed by a colleague, usually someone who is working as a garda informant.

SEXTASY; ecstasy and Viagra taken together.

SHAFT, TO; to betray.

SHAG, TO; to have sex.

SHAKEDOWN, TO; garda slang used to describe a thorough search for criminals.

SHARK; a gambler.

SHIT; another name for heroin.

SHITBOX; the anus.

SHITFACED; a term applied to someone who is high on drugs or drunk.

SHIT-FOR-BRAINS; a stupid person.

SHOOTER; a gunman.

SHOOTING GALLERY; a location where heroin addicts converge.

SHOOT UP, TO; to inject heroin.

SHORT, A; a handgun.

SHUT-EYE; sleep.

SKANK; a form of herbal cannabis.

SKIN POPPING; to inject a drug beneath the skin.

SKIN TRADE; used to describe the world of prostitution.

SKINT; to be penniless.

SKIN-UP; to roll a cannabis cigarette.

SKUNK; a hybrid form of cannabis plant.

SLAG; a promiscuous woman.

SLAMMER; a prison.

SLAP AND TICKLE; a sexual liaison.

SLAPPER; a young promiscuous girl.

SLOP OUT, TO; cleaning out urine and faeces from a prison cell bucket.

SLOSH, TO; to urinate.

SMACK; heroin.

SNOUT; a garda informer.

SNOW; cocaine.

SNUFF MOVIE; a film which shows the death of a participant, often after they have been sexually abused.

Space cadet, a; habitual user of drugs.

Spaced out; to be under the influence of drugs.

Spanking the monkey; masturbating.

Special, the; criminal and garda slang for the Special Criminal Court, a non-jury court which hears terrorism and organised crime trials.

Special K; ketamine.

Speed; amphetamines.

Speedball; a mixture of heroin and cocaine.

Speedballing; to shoot up or smoke a mixture of cocaine and heroin.

Spliff, a; a cigarette that contains cannabis.

Spondulas; street name for money.

Spring, to; to help a prison inmate to escape.

Squeal, to; to inform.

Squeeze; to exert pressure.

Stake out; term given to a garda operation where police mount a covert surveillance operation to detect a crime.

Stall, to; to delay.

Stardust; cocaine.

Stash, a; a secret location where drugs or guns are hidden.

Sticky fingers; criminal slang for someone who is prone to stealing.

Stiff, to; to murder someone.

Stiff, a; a body.

Sting; a confidence trick.

Sting operation; controlled delivery of drugs to a criminal gang by the security forces or customs.

STONED; to be under the influence of drugs.

STONER, A; a person who uses drugs.

STRAIGHT; to desist from engaging in crime. To go straight.

STREETWALKER; garda term applied to prostitutes who solicit clients in public places.

SUPERGRASS; a criminal or paramilitary who agrees to testify in court against his former associates.

SWAG; the proceeds of a robbery or drug deal.

SWALLOWER AND STUFFER; a drugs courier who conceals drugs inside their body.

SWEETENER; a bribe.

SWINDLER; a fraudster.

TAB; to keep tabs on someone; to monitor them from a distance. Also an ecstasy tablet.

TAIL, TO; to follow, or a surveillance unit.

TAKE A GANDER; to look at or to inspect.

TAKE THE RAP; to accept responsibility or to admit to a crime.

TALK, TO; to co-operate with gardaí.

TANK; a police or prison cell.

TANK UP; to get drunk.

TARGET ONE; nickname given to Curtis Warren, a drugs trafficker reputed to be the biggest dealer in Europe.

THAI STICKS; cannabis sticks which are soaked in oil.

TIP-OFF; confidential information given to gardaí.

TOAST; to be killed.

TOD, TO BE ON YOUR; to be alone.

TOE-RAG; someone who is strongly disliked.

TOMMY; criminal slang for a machine-gun.

TOP, TO; to murder.

TOP OFF, TO; to kill.

TORCH, TO; to burn down.

TOSSER; a fool.

TOUT; a garda informer.

TRACKER-KNACKER; a working-class person who wears tracksuits.

TRACK MARKS; scars usually left on the arms of intravenous drug users.

TRACKS; fingerprints.

TRIADS; name given to Chinese gangs who organise prostitution, gambling and knife fights; triads are heavily involved in extortion.

TRICK; a sex act.

TRIGGER MAN; a criminal who murders people for criminal gangs.

TRIP, A; a drug-related experience.

TURF; territory controlled by a criminal gang.

TURN A TRICK; to commit a crime; to perform a sexual act.

TURN OVER; to raid a property or business premises.

TURN UP THE HEAT; to exert pressure on a criminal.

TURNED ON; sexually aroused.

U.C.Bs ; under-car bombs are improvised explosive devices which are placed underneath cars and designed to kill the occupants.

UDA; the Ulster Defence Association, a loyalist paramilitary group.

UNDERWORLD; the world of organised crime, fraud, violence and drug trafficking.

UNKIE; morphine.

UP THE POLE; pregnant.

UPPERS AND DOWNERS; slang for amphetamines and barbiturates.

USER; a drug taker.

UVF; the Ulster Volunteer Force, a loyalist paramilitary group established in 1966 in response to a rise in Irish nationalism.

UZI; criminal slang for an Uzi 9-mm sub-machine-gun.

VERBALS; an oral confession.

VICE; the world of prostitution.

VIGGO; slang word used by both gardaí and criminals to describe community activists who oppose drug dealers. It is an abbreviation of the word 'vigilante'.

VITAMIN K; ketamine.

VOLUNTEER; term used by paramilitaries to describe their members.

WAGON; criminal slang for a garda van.

WALK-IN; a criminal who enters a police station to confess to a crime.

WASH MONEY, TO; to launder money by putting it through a series of transactions until its illegal source can no longer be traced.

WASTED; to be high on drugs.

WCCs; white collar criminals. The term is also used to describe crimes committed by professional people.

WEED; cannabis.

WELL-HEELED; having plenty of money.

WHACK, TO; to murder someone.

WHITE; cocaine.

WHITE LADY; cocaine.

WHITE STUFF; cocaine.

WHIZZ; amphetamines.

WHORE; a prostitute. It is also used to describe a woman who sleeps around.

WHOREHOUSE; a brothel or a location where prostitutes service customers.

WIPE AN EYE; to deceive.

WIPE OUT; to murder.

WITCH; cocaine or heroin.

WORKS; street slang for syringes and other paraphernalia used to take heroin and crack cocaine.

X; ecstasy.

YANK YOUR CHAIN; to pull a fast one, or to deceive someone.

YARDIE; member of a Jamaican criminal gang.

YELLOW; someone who is inexperienced or afraid.

YFGs; Yugoslavian Fragmentation Grenade.

YOBBO; a violent person.

YOKE; an ecstasy tablet.

Z; an ounce of heroin.

ZOMBIE; a drug addict.

ZOO, THE; Mountjoy Prison in Dublin.

Sources

BOOKS

Green, J. *The Slang Thesaurus* (1988). Penguin.

Kearse, R. *Street Talk. Da Official Guide to Hip-Hop & Urban Slanguage.* (2006). Barricade Books.

Monteleone, V. *Criminal Slang: The Vernacular of the Underground Lingo.* (2004) The Lawbook Exchange.

Morton, J. *Gangster Speak. A Dictionary of Criminal and Sexual slang.* (2006). Virgin Books.

Peckham, A. *Mo' Urban Dictionary, Ridonkulous Street Slang Defined.* (2007). Andrews McMeel Publishing.

INTERNET

http://www.pride.org/slangdrugterms.htm
http://www.peevish.co.uk/slang